How to make Robot move like a Human with Reinforcement Learning.

From the authors of the leading algorithm on the Open-AI's leaderboard. 2nd edition.

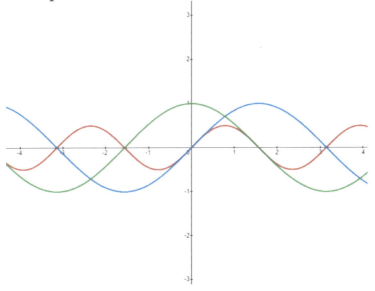

Timur Ishuov, Michele Folgheraiter,

Abdubakir Qo'shboqov, Zhenis Otarbay,

Madi Nurmanov

Contents

Preface:

This concise book contains the most important basis of the "Symphony" algorithm. As a painter or composer removes unimportant parts, so did the author, removing most of the intermediate less beneficial concepts.

This book is intended to students or researchers who are interested in Reinforcement Learning, specifically, in Off-policy Actor and Critic based continuous algorithms. But it also contains direct implementation of the logic in python with explanations for beginners to understand.

Dedicated to my mom Pakhitkanym, wife Saya and sister Zhanna, and my kids Abylai and Kyzdanai. I am thankful to my God, Jesus Christ, forever and beyond.

The Flowers: How beautiful they are?

Rectified Huber Error loss function:

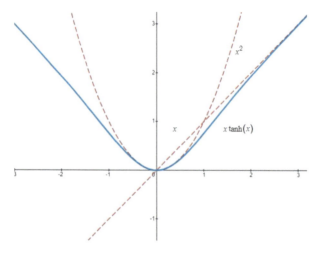

This particular function, which shares similarities with Huber Error, was discovered during desire to jump faster to the desired gradient with the naive idea of increasing the speed of learning in the end (A is desired gradient):

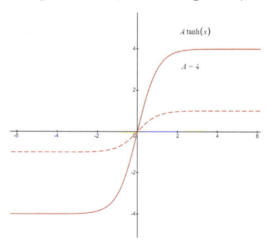

But instead of improving learning it would improve the error level as gradient often has a high level of the noise especially in the beginning

Surprisingly enough, the function abs(x)tanh(x) appeared first. We wanted to limit the gradient to its own absolute value. How pathetic were we? To our surprise, with this function when applied specifically to Return Loss, the Reinforcement Learning agent was learning faster. It is asymmetrical which suits asymmetrical Reward function.

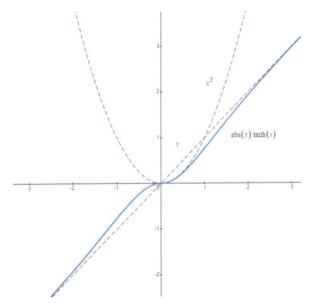

Considering Reinforcement Learning, outliers or strong incorrect errors when squared can direct the agent to undesired policies, but on the other hand, strong correct errors can bring faster convergence to desired policies. If early stoppage is applied or convergence is loosened somehow, squared error (x^2 on the graph) in the faultless simulation environment, does not bring apparent drawback for the agent's learning (only you need to consider that real world is not a "vacuum").

Particular advantage this function brings when applied to "real" Loss function or error between prediction and target instead of direct Q value based policy update: When reward is between 0.0 and 1.0, predicted Return or Q value is usually in units or dozens, hence with abs(x)tanh(x) there is no clear dynamics utilization. But when we subtract a new predicted Q value from the previously predicted Q value (detached from graph, averaged and stored), the true miracle starts to happen (Q value can be too strong and volatile in comparison with delta or Advantage).

Usually the mentioned difference has an embedded noise factor due to prediction errors, often policy can fluctuate because of the accumulation of these errors. This problem is getting worse when we have unstable agents like Humanoid. But as this noise is dumped/squashed in abs(x)tanh(x) for lower values and has an identity relationship for stronger values, we have an agent that approaches desired policy much smoother and faster. Comparison of the version x*tanh(x/2):

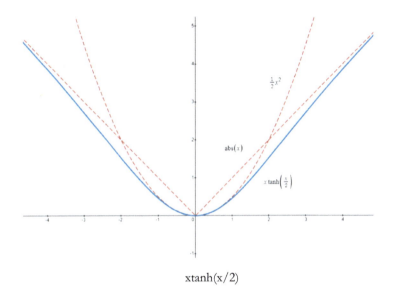

$$x\tanh(x/2)$$

with the original Huber Loss:

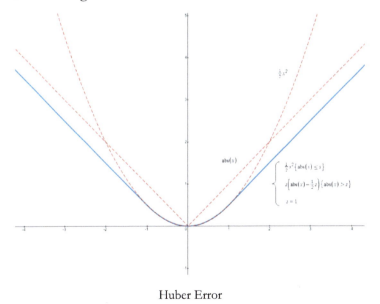

Huber Error

Another option is to decrease reward if it lies between 0.0 and 1.0 by 100 to 200 in order to bring Return or Q value to normalized level. Which was used in one of the first implementations. In this case benefits of the activation function holds. However, volatility problem is not completely solved (we used tanh on Q value to diminish volatility of the "tail")

Finally, we applied symmetrical xtanh(x) to the convergence of Q value or Critic, and asymmetrical abs(x)tanh(x) to the convergence of Advantage function or Actor/Policy.

Implementation of xtanh(x) and abs(x)tanh(x):

```python
#Rectified Hubber Error Loss Function
def ReHE(error):
    ae = torch.abs(error).mean()
    return ae*torch.tanh(ae)

#Rectified Hubber Assymetric Error Loss Function
def ReHAE(error):
    e = error.mean()
    return torch.abs(e)*torch.tanh(e)
```

We call them Rectified Huber Error(ReHE) and Rectified Huber Assymetrical Error (ReHAE) Loss Functions

Script below shows the Actor's update with Advantage. Advantage is a key factor in favor of assymetric abs(x)*tanh(x) Loss Function (ReHAE). Notice that Advantage is negative, so that it should increase, or Loss Function turns into Reward Function:

```
def actor_update(self, state):
    action = self.actor(state, mean=True)
    q_new_policy = self.critic(state, action, united=True)
    actor_loss = -(q_new_policy - self.q_old_policy)

    actor_loss = ReHAE(actor_loss)

    self.actor_optimizer.zero_grad()
    actor_loss.backward(retain_graph=True)
    self.actor_optimizer.step()

    with torch.no_grad():
        self.q_old_policy = q_new_policy.mean().detach()

    return q_new_policy.mean()
```

Update 2nd Edition:

Advantage or Delta above is the difference between current prediction of Q values and previous prediction of Q variance without dependency on the considered State. It compares samples of the Dataset or Replay Buffer taking into account big batch size and average between samples: new samples should produce better Qs.

Another possibility is the A2C type update, when Advantage or Delta between the current prediction and the previous prediction of Q values at the current State is considered. But A2C is on-policy algorithm without target networks and replay buffer (log probability*Advatage). Usage of Target Critic could make Delta and its variance consequently bigger.

We are going to show the latest version of the Symphony algorithm.

Symphony: Music of Gestures

It all started from an exploration noise. The exploration noise is often an issue. Some algorithms subtly increase the exploration noise (SAC), some have a latent noise (TD3). In the past we had some experience with Fourier Series, and understood that they could adjust to any function and be a function approximator's alternative. However, the number of components with increase in dimension (x1, x2, x3...) rise exponentially. But the number of components is not an issue for neural networks. Instead of the original state, we decided to apply cos(state), sin(state) and cos(state)sin(state) concatenation as unit building blocks for the neural network to approximate. It can be considered as harmonical noise and make a positive effect on exploration.

F[f(x)]

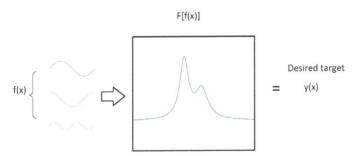

$f(x)$

Desired target

$=$ $y(x)$

Without these functions, having pure state as an input to the function approximator, an unbalanced agent (natural noise is coming from agent's unbalanced state, would not work for balanced agents) learns very fast how to move forward (the algorithm is Actor-Critic in the form of "careful" TD3, which takes element-wise minimum of 3 networks predictions, will be shown later). It moves accurately with small gradient steps, not falling and producing astonishing unseen values of 20,000-30,000 average scores if not limited by time steps. But if put in the real-world conditions from the simulation vacuum, it can fall from a wind blow.

Function Approximator now instead of approximating the target using variable x as an input, approximates it using harmonical functions of x. It needs to deduce x from the system of f(x). This approach can be called function learning functions.

"Miracle" here is that input functions do not integrate white or gaussian noise. They follow periodic functions rules and have a clear dependency between f(x) and x. According to the Fourier series most functions can be described by sin and cos functions of different amplitude and frequency. And here is a very rough approximation to it. It lacks frequency factor:

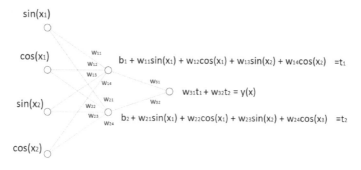

Original Multilayer Perceptron based neural networks have a similar problem, they lack order of polynomials (x2, x3, etc.) considering Taylor series in the input.

Now, we came to the Music of Gestures. What if harmonics are inside neural networks, not outside of them?

We decided to rewrite Linear Layer to Fourier Transform. We started from the clear form:

When input is multiplied by the weight, the weight becomes a frequency. Then if it is multiplied by the following weight, it becomes amplitude, and if bias is added -voila! – we have a constant part. And all is learned:

$$\sin(w_1x_1)$$

$$w_1$$

$$x_1 \quad w_2 \quad \cos(w_2x_1) \quad w_{11}$$

$$w_{12}$$

$$x_2 \quad w_3 \quad \sin(w_3x_2) \quad w_{13} \quad b_1 + w_{11}\sin(w_1x_1) + w_{12}\cos(w_2x_1) + w_{13}\cos(w_3x_2) + w_{14}\cos(w_4x_2) = y(x)$$

$$w_{14}$$

$$w_4$$

$$\cos(w_4x_2)$$

With the perceptron at the end:

$$\sin(w_1x_1)$$

$$w_1$$

$$x_1 \quad w_2 \quad \cos(w_2x_1) \quad w_{11}$$

$$w_{12}$$

$$w_{13}$$

$$b_1 + w_{11}\sin(w_1x_1) + w_{12}\cos(w_2x_1) + w_{13}\cos(w_3x_2) + w_{14}\cos(w_4x_2) = t_1$$

$$w_{14} \quad w_{31}$$

$$x_2 \quad w_3 \quad \sin(w_3x_2) \quad w_{52}$$

$$w_{31}t_1 + w_{32}t_2 = y(x)$$

$$w_{21} \quad w_{52}$$

$$w_{22}$$

$$w_4 \quad w_{23} \quad b_2 + w_{21}\sin(w_1x_1) + w_{22}\cos(w_2x_1) + w_{23}\cos(w_3x_2) + w_{24}\cos(w_4x_2) = t_2$$

$$w_{24}$$

$$\cos(w_4x_2)$$

Now the function has frequency, amplitude, and bias factors which Fourier Series requires.

Finishing touch is a fully connected linear layer with input and output neurons and weight matrix. For simplicity we removed the cosine part but added bias to the sine part.

And these, on the contrary, improved the network, cause with bias we had all different phases available.

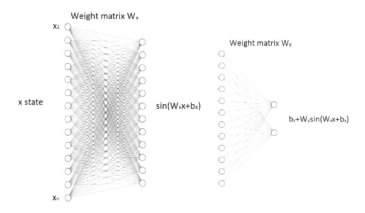

Implementation:

```
class FourierTransform(nn.Module):
    def __init__(self, f_in, f_out):
        super().__init__()
        limit = np.sqrt(2 / float(f_in+f_out))
        self.weights = nn.Parameter(torch.normal(torch.zeros(f_in, f_out), std=limit))
        self.bias = nn.Parameter(torch.normal(torch.zeros(f_out), std=limit))


    def forward(self, input):
        x = torch.matmul(input, self.weights)+ self.bias
        return torch.sin(x)
```

Inside network:

```
self.net = nn.Sequential(
    nn.Linear(state_dim, hidden_dim),
    nn.LayerNorm(hidden_dim),
    FourierTransform(hidden_dim, hidden_dim),
    nn.LeakyReLU(0.1),
    nn.Linear(hidden_dim, action_dim),
    nn.Tanh()
)
```

As was found out Fourier series Linear Layer requires excessive training, otherwise it converges like a "striking bolt" at the beginning but then deviates due to harmonical instability (untrained noise). It is discussed in the next section.

Update 2nd Edition:

The latest update is simplified to 2 consecutive Linear Layers and rectified Sine activation in between:

```python
class ReSine(nn.Module):
    def forward(self, x):
        return F.leaky_relu(torch.sin(x), 0.1)


class FourierSeries(nn.Module):
    def __init__(self, hidden_dim, f_out):
        super().__init__()


        self.fft = nn.Sequential(
            nn.Linear(hidden_dim, hidden_dim),
            ReSine(),
            nn.Linear(hidden_dim, f_out)
        )

    def forward(self, x):
        return self.fft(x)
```

Inside Actor's module. The "action" method does not have Gaussian Noise, but some periodic varying disturbance – to not destroy gears/motors/shafts:

```python
# Define the actor network
class Actor(nn.Module):
    def __init__(self, state_dim, action_dim, device, hidden_dim=32,
                 max_action=1.0, ou_process = False):

        super(Actor, self).__init__()

        self.input = Input(state_dim, hidden_dim)

        self.net = nn.Sequential(
            FourierSeries(hidden_dim, action_dim),
            nn.Tanh()
        )

        self.max_action = torch.mean(max_action).item()
        self.disturbance = Disturbance(action_dim, max_action, device, ou_process)

    def forward(self, state):
        x = self.input(state)
        x = self.max_action*self.net(x)
        x += (0.07*torch.randn_like(x)).clamp(-0.175, 0.175)
        return x.clamp(-self.max_action, self.max_action)


    def action(self, state):
        with torch.no_grad():
            x = self.input(state)
            x = self.max_action*self.net(x)
            x += self.disturbance.generate()
        return x.clamp(-self.max_action, self.max_action)
```

It is convenient to separate Forward implementation for Actor's update during training which has some subtle Gaussian Noise, and Action generation without gradient calculation for the Environment step – which may not have Gaussian Noise or Stochastic Probability Distribution (for practical reasons), but some smooth disturbance.

18

Ocean: Let me walk upon the waters

Imagine the simplest scenario, you have a State that consists only of 1 parameter, and you have only 1 continuous Action. A better reward is given depending on the State and Action parameter.

If we have small Gaussian Noise or Small Probability Distribution for actions, the State and Action exploration area will be narrow, toward highest gradient, but we could easily miss better Actor behavior or Policy.

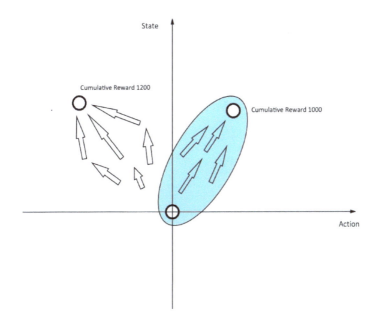

Instead, what we want is:

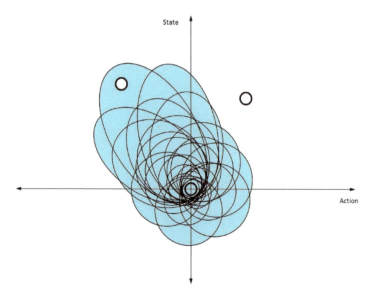

In 2017, Bellemare suggested searching for better Qs through learning Q distribution simultaneously with learning Q. Doing so, could result in generating different solutions.

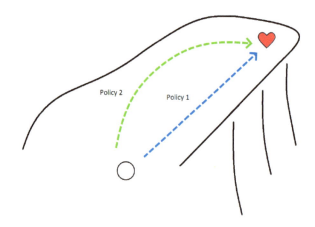

Bellemare hinted at using the Bellman equation to calculate variance (adjusted gamma position).

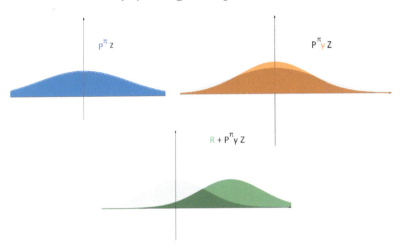

But the reward has its own small distribution, and the more correct form is to do:

$$\delta^2{}_Q = \delta^2{}_r + COV(r,\ Qt') + \gamma^2\, \delta^2{}_{Qt'}$$

However, we can neglect the covariance part because 1 step reward distribution is almost totally uncorrelated to long-run Q value or Return distribution, but to consider that there should be a very small correlation, we can program covariance to be $(\gamma - \gamma^2)\delta^2{}_{Qt'}$ and for $\gamma = 0.99$ it is $0.18\, \delta^2{}_{Qt'}$. Most importantly the equation can be simplified to the Bellman operator:

$$\delta^2{}_Q = \delta^2{}_r + \gamma\, \delta^2{}_{Qt'}$$

Which is in code:

```
def critic_update(self, state, action, reward, next_state, done):

    with torch.no_grad():
        for target_param, param in zip(self.critic_target.parameters(), self.critic.parameters()):
            target_param.data.copy_(0.997*target_param.data + 0.003*param)

        next_action = self.actor(next_state)
        q_next_target, s2_next_target = self.critic_target(next_state, next_action, united=True)
        q_value = reward + (1-done) * 0.99 * q_next_target
        s2_value = torch.var(reward) + (1-done) * 0.99 * s2_next_target
```

This is not 100% correct, but the Q network will "program" correlation that we agreed on.

There is one important moment, usually 1 step reward is normalized between -1.0 and 1.0. When the value is big, e.g. 10 or 100, its variance usually is equal or smaller than the value, usually.

This is not always the case, but can hold for Gaussian Distribution:

But for normalized value, the variance can be bigger than the value itself, e.g. for the average 0.1 the variance can be 0.5.

Learning with Bellman Operator will make Q variance even bigger through accumulation of the reward's variance. It in turn will result in more prevalence of distribution learning than Q learning. Which can be beneficial, but also can make the agent search for bad policies in the beginning, especially if we increase Q and Q distribution synchronously through an actor's update.

The most obvious solution (apart from increasing reward) is to dump reward variance (approx. from 1e-2 to 1e-3) and to decrease accumulated sum or Bellman operator (approx. from 1e-2 to 1e-3). The latter is needed because, when initialized, Q target network will produce values close to zero, but not dumped, which will result in overestimation.

```python
def critic_update(self, state, action, reward, next_state, done):

    with torch.no_grad():
        for target_param, param in zip(self.critic_target.parameters(), self.critic.parameters()):
            target_param.data.copy_(0.997*target_param.data + 0.003*param)

        next_action = self.actor(next_state)
        q_next_target, s2_next_target = self.critic_target(next_state, next_action, united=True)
        q_value = reward + (1-done) * 0.99 * q_next_target
        s2_value = 3e-2 * (3e-2 * torch.var(reward) + (1-done) * 0.99 * s2_next_target)

    out = self.critic(state, action, united=False)
    critic_loss = ReHE(q_value - out[0]) + ReHE(q_value - out[1]) + ReHE(q_value - out[2]) + ReHE(s2_value - out[3])

    self.critic_optimizer.zero_grad()
    critic_loss.backward()
    self.critic_optimizer.step()

    return next_action
```

* The argument "united" in Q network when True, will produce an element-wise minimum of 3 subnets, otherwise separate outputs:

```python
# Define the critic network
class Critic(nn.Module):
    def __init__(self, state_dim, action_dim, hidden_dim=32):
        super(Critic, self).__init__()

        self.input = Input(state_dim+action_dim, hidden_dim)

        qA = FourierSeries(hidden_dim, 1)
        qB = FourierSeries(hidden_dim, 1)
        qC = FourierSeries(hidden_dim, 1)

        s2 = FourierSeries(hidden_dim, 1)

        self.nets = nn.ModuleList([qA, qB, qC, s2])

    def forward(self, state, action, united=False):
        x = torch.cat([state, action], -1)
        x = self.input(x)
        xs = [net(x) for net in self.nets]
        if not united: return xs
        stack = torch.stack(xs[:3], dim=-1)
        return torch.min(stack, dim=-1).values, xs[3]
```

Accessories: Details matter

Image from Freepick.com

As is known from the Neural Networks learning, hyperparameters can drastically change the behavior of the network: large scale networks behave differently than smaller ones, the replay buffer with priority weights makes a distributional shift, etc.

As was mentioned, we used a slight modification of the Twin Delayed DDPG algorithm or TD3. While TD3 uses 2 Critics and takes minimum between 2 predictions, during experiments it was proven that gradient update stepwise should be as small as possible (we make computing work easier for our optimizer), the strongest approach was to use element-wise minimum between 3 predictions.

In this book we wanted to pay some attention to the replay buffer used. It is in between original experience replay buffer and replay buffer with importance sampling. It assigns priorities linearly considering history, but squashes priorities with factor 0.001. In this case distribution does not change too much, but we move - moving produces life – otherwise the original replay buffer is a stack type memory before it reaches its capacity, then it becomes a simple moving average, in between sudden distributional change happens. And the computational cost of indexes as weights is less than with Importance Sampling:

```python
def sample(self):

    indexes = np.array(list(range(self.length)))
    weights = 0.001*(indexes/self.length)
    probs = weights/np.sum(weights)

    batch_indices = self.random.choice(indexes, p=probs, size=self.batch_size)
    batch = [self.buffer[indx-1] for indx in batch_indices]
    states, actions, rewards, next_states, dones = map(np.vstack, zip(*batch))
```

The hidden layer size is 256.

The batch size is increasing from 128 to 1000. The idea of the sample in statistics is to describe the population. Imagine how a 256 sized sample can still describe the population of 1mln? For the policy to not deviate from the expectation we increase the sample size

Also, a very crucial idea for creating human-like motion is to focus on balancing first and then to move forward: we recommend limiting the number of steps an agent undertakes in the beginning but increase it exponentially with time. Particularly we used this equation:

$$\text{clip\_steps} = \text{steps}_{avg} + 15$$

where steps_{avg} = average number of steps of last 100 episodes.

Finally, we wanted to explain harmonical instability. We don't use external noise. Noise that appears at the beginning and in the future is due to undertrained harmonical (oscillatory) state of the Fourier based neural networks. For input values that change linearly especially at the beginning it creates oscillations, and if the model is not trained fast it can diverge. We do from 50 to 200 step training between episodes and 2-3 step training at each frame/interactive step.

Update 2e edition. We added exploratory noise produced by Ornstein–Uhlenbeck process but instead of complementary Gaussian Distribution we added a varying gradually changing signal. Gaussian Noise or Exploratory noise in general tends to burst the learning process. However Stochastic Gaussian Noise can cause gears, shafts, and motors to break down earlier.

Considering environments where there are hard obstacles, it is also important to add some reward for state change in between transitions, as there is a punishment for the torque application, we balance it to give additional reward for moving. Otherwise, the agent decides that it is much safer to stand still than to move forward. This concept was called "Movement is Life and Stalling is dangerous" due to logarithmic/exponential scale. The reward calculation is embedded in the Replay Buffer:

```
#moving is life, stalling is dangerous
delta = np.mean(np.abs(next_state - state)).clip(1e-1, 10.0)
reward -= self.stall_penalty*math.log10(1.0/delta)
```

We wanted to show the training procedure with A2C type update. We use Next Action produced by the Actor network during Critic's Update to save time, and Next State stored in the Replay Buffer due to State-Action-Reward-Next State transitions:

```
def train(self, batch):
    state, action, reward, next_state, done = batch
    next_action = self.critic_update(state, action, reward, next_state, done)
    return self.actor_update(next_state, next_action)

def critic_update(self, state, action, reward, next_state, done):

    with torch.no_grad():
        for target_param, param in zip(self.critic_target.parameters(), self.critic.parameters()):
            target_param.data.copy_(0.997*target_param.data + 0.003*param)

        next_action = self.actor(next_state)
        q_next_target, s2_next_target = self.critic_target(next_state, next_action, united=True)
        q_value = reward + (1-done) * 0.99 * q_next_target
        s2_value = 3e-2 * (3e-2 * torch.var(reward) + (1-done) * 0.99 * s2_next_target)

    out = self.critic(state, action, united=False)
    critic_loss = ReHE(q_value - out[0]) + ReHE(q_value - out[1]) + ReHE(q_value - out[2]) + ReHE(s2_value - out[3])

    self.critic_optimizer.zero_grad()
    critic_loss.backward()
    self.critic_optimizer.step()

    return next_action

def actor_update(self, next_state, next_action):
    with torch.no_grad():
        next_q_old_policy, next_s2_old_policy = self.critic(next_state, next_action, united=True)
        next_q_old_policy, next_s2_old_policy = next_q_old_policy.mean().detach(), next_s2_old_policy.mean().detach()

    next_action = self.actor(next_state)
    next_q_new_policy, next_s2_new_policy = self.critic(next_state, next_action, united=True)
    actor_loss = -ReHaE(next_q_new_policy - next_q_old_policy) -ReHaE(next_s2_new_policy - next_s2_old_policy)

    self.actor_optimizer.zero_grad()
    actor_loss.backward()
    self.actor_optimizer.step()

    return actor_loss
```

Both Actor's updates, original one and A2C type one have its one objective. It is possible to unite both. The first one is much faster in the beginning, but the latter one more canonical and with a clear objective – compare Q at the current State, while the first compares Q on average.

Symbiosis: Uniting opposites

Image from Freepick.com

There is a possibility to add Monte-Carlo experiment to Temporal Difference learning if the agent does not require high level of balancing. We call this algorithm a concept, it allowed us to solve Bipedal Walker environment within 100 episodes.

The idea is to do 1 step update using Monte-Carlo collected samples, and 1 step update via Temporal Difference prediction. The roll-out is constituted by n-steps (200) and is collected at each step and after done to have "a full-length roll-out" for each step.

One corrects another: since stored rollouts are limited in number at the beginning and clipped by n-steps (200), we assure ourselves that Temporal Difference equation holds; at the same time, the next target prediction can be erroneous, learning based on Monte-Carlo experiments helps us to avoid that.

If the terminal reward occurs, it is divided by n steps. As we neglect done, (1-done) factor is removed from Bellman's Temporal Difference equation. Reward itself is divided by n steps, so that Return for n steps can be less than 1.0 due to gamma multiplier (by Return we assume Q Value, we use them interchangeably). We can also say that Return is approximately normalized between -1 and 1. For additional guarantee, we also squash the tail of the Return by tanh function.

Fading Memory

As old transitions contain Returns from old policies, and the exact same transition could contain different Return if it is recalculated at the current time step, we need to neglect old transitions as time goes on. And we do it gradually, sampling with priorities regarding history.

Distributional Perspective

Since we have access to real Return data, it would be remiss not to improve variance (when dealing with numbers lower than 1.0 variance is less than standard deviation by its own value, 0.1*0.1=0.01). Especially when one has Adam like adaptive optimizer that has variable speed and consequently acceleration. While if started from 0.0, algorithm based on the temporal difference learns gradually (when target network slowly follows prediction network), Monte-Carlo based supervised learning algorithm can jump immediately towards the highest gradient. One can use a gradient clipping method like Proximal Policy Optimization. Another approach is to learn and improve variance when improving Return. When we have a bigger variance, we can be guaranteed that we found different paths to do the same task and we are not following the steepest gradient.

If for Monte-Carlo update, variance can be directly derived from Return sample, for the Temporal Difference update, one can do sum of variances:

$$\delta^2_Q = \delta^2_r + COV(r,\ Qt') + \gamma^2\, \delta^2_{Qt'}.$$

We neglect the covariance part because 1 step reward distribution is almost totally uncorrelated to 200 step Return distribution, but to consider that there should be a very small correlation, we program covariance as: $(\gamma - \gamma^2)\delta^2_{Qt'}$, so that:

$$\delta^2_Q = \delta^2_r + \gamma\, \delta^2_{Qt'}.$$

The reward function was important when combining two updates. Simple sum of Return and variance could lead to ambiguous proportions, while simple multiplication could lead to vanishing gradients due to Return being minimized to very small numbers, while variance of it if even smaller. So, we used the following equation as Policy Reward function:

$$\exp(-Q)*\exp(-\delta^2) \text{ or the equivalent, } \exp(-Q-\delta^2)$$

This function is an exponential decay, to approach zero it requires argument to increase. Now both factors are dependent on each other. One cannot increase without pushing the other to increase.

Policy Loss function: $-\exp(-Q-\delta^2)$

About the authors:

Timur Ishuov
First Author
University of Szeged
PhD candidate

Dr. Michele Folgheraiter
Co-author
Nazarbayev University
Associate Professor

Abdubakir Qo'shboqov
Editor
University of Szeged
PhD candidate

Zhenis Otarbay
Contributor
Nazarbayev University
PhD candidate

Madi Nurmanov
Contributor
Ecole centrale de Nantes
Msc Eng

Open your fingers
wiggle and chat

any age
Anytime
recognized all over the world

with laughter and smile
up, down, sideways

to the sides
round

enthusiastically
rhythmically
uncontrollably

dance

to the music of gestures